VILLAINY

VILLAINY

ANDREA ABI-KARAM

NIGHTBOAT BOOKS

NEW YORK

Copyright © 2021 by Andrea Abi-Karam
Printed in the United States

ISBN: 978-1-64362-110-4

Cover photo of author by Lix Z, 2021. Courtesy of the artist.
Design and Typesetting by NOR Research Studio
Text set in Komu and Perpetua

Cataloging-in-publication data is available from the Library of Congress

Nightboat Books
New York
www.nightboat.org

for those who were taken too soon

we need to open a revolutionary terrain for the invention of new organs
& desires, for which no pleasure has yet been defined
—— Paul B. Preciado

Bodies fray at their limits. At their limits, they become indistinguishable
——Tiqqun

yeahhh they really want you they really want you & I do too
—— Hole

and I had to come, & I had to die
—— Kevin Killian

THE END OF FASCISM LOOKS LIKE CENTURIES OF QUEERS DANCING ON THE GRAVE OF

1. CAPITALISM
2. THE STATE
3. COLONIALISM
4. NAZIS
5. RACISM
6. OPPRESSION

IT WILL BE A GRAND PARTY EVEN GRANDER THAN MARDI
GRAS & THERE WILL BE NO REASON TO SLEEP B/C THERE WILL
BE NO NEED TO WORK & THERE WILL BE SUCH A REVELATORY
PALLOR TO THE WHOLE THING THE PHOTOS WILL BE
EXQUISITE & THE LIBATIONS & SNACKS FUCKING DELICIOUS
THERE WILL BE A GIANT DANCE PARTY & CLUB CHAI WILL DJ &
IT WILL BE AT THE STUD & WE'LL ALL FUCKING DANCE UNTIL
WE SWEAT HARD & MAKEUP RUNS BETWEEN FACES
A TRANSFERENCE
A TRANSFUSION OF GLAM

A FUSION OF SWEATING BODIES INTO A WHATEVER
SINGULARITY A TRANSFUSION OUT OF A FUCKING OPPRESSED
MISERABLE EXISTENCE INTO A REVELRY A FULL BLOWN
REVELRY OF QUEERNESS & DESIRE THAT WE HAVE ONLY NOW
JUST BARELY BEGUN TO IMAGINE
JUST BARELY BEGUN TO IMAGINE
JUST BARELY BEGUN TO IMAGINE

You fuck me with your entire hand in a room full of the dead. The dead are inside boxes behind glass. You fuck me so we can feel for one second that our friends are not dead. That they are living inside of us. A security guard approaches & you stop. I pull you up from the floor by the lapels of your leather jacket. Face covered in cum. I exhale & absorb our dead friends into my body like you opened up a gateway for their arrival. I absorb them into my body & hope they will stay. & that they are happy & dry & warm. I give up the possibility of sleep for myself in an effort to make an environment for my dead friends. A social space. A closed world.

a slow song comes on. it's called the leaving song. the crowd pushes forward but there is no longer a forward to brake into. the crowd tries anyway until my feet are no longer on the floor & your feet are no longer on the floor & I press my hand against your cock while I am pressed against so many other people & so many other people are pressed against you/ some of them are the same & some of them are just more & our feet are off the ground. you are moaning. some of the mass is concerned that you are going to pass out that the possibility of (a singularity unbecoming) unbecoming a singularity is beyond the present. is too soon. our feet are off the ground. the crowd pushes forward your cum covers my hand the others pressed against me cover the back of my neck in sweat you begin to fall & I pull you up so you don't fall beneath the feet of the expanded self

I'm horny as fuck so I find another queer on the internet & they drive
an hour to meet me. two & a half strong 6 packs later we go on a walk.
they've been talking the entire time. we go on a walk for cigarettes &
I take you to a park at a dead end next to the freeway. I lay my leather
jacket down under a tree & you anxiously dig through your bag for
gloves & lube. you say you want to top me but clearly you're too
anxious. you start to fuck me under the tree. what I want is to be fucked
out of reality. we are in the park where I went to a friend's memorial a
couple months ago & I just want to be fucked out of tragedy so I don't
have to think anymore/so I don't have to think about place or self or
context/or how I met you on the internet & you definitely talk too
much/I want to think about unbecoming. you fuck me with lube &
gloves & not enough fingers & not enough confidence. I regret taking
you somewhere previously occupied by another memory. now it isn't the
park at the end of the block where I went to a memorial/it's the park
where all I wanted was to unbecome & you couldn't give that to me so
now every time I walk by I remember how I am unfulfilled/how my
friends' lives are unfulfilled/because they're over/how high quality lube
isn't enough to erase the fact that this is also where I tried to celebrate
the dead & now the dead are covered in high quality lube that never got
pushed far enough inside me/that they are dead/that this is the ground
slightly damp/that this is a vista for the freeway/that this is the vantage
point between the port [global capitalism] & a pile of trash where a
cement playground used to be. you don't give me enough of yourself
& too soon you want to go get more beer & then drive the two hours
home. I beg you to drink water & sleep for a while so you don't crash on
the way home. the list of my dead friends began with a crash. although

6

you had part of your timid hand inside me you don't count as a friend but I still do not want you to die. you drive off anyway/directions back to sacramento written on your hand with a purple glitter pen. I should have gone for a run.

you have a panic attack because an abusive ex roommate master tenant landlord keeps showing up places I have a panic attack because I'm afraid of the party I'm afraid of the future I literally cannot stop freaking out & anxiety writing feels alright & anxiety fucking feels even better

I WANT A BETTER APOCALYPSE THIS ONE SUCKS

SO WHY DON'T U JUST

FUCK ME OUT OF REALITY

THE AFTERMATH
15

AN UNBECOMING
29

WHAT IS CLOSED/ WHAT IS CONTAINED
51

I GOT LOST/I GOT DELETED
61

THE PARALLEL BETWEEN BODY & EARTH
71

THE INTERRUPTION VS BLOCKADE
75

TEMPORARY / AUTONOMOUS / DESIRE
89

"POETRY AS FORCES"
115

THE AFTERMATH

there's a way in which american literature

pretends to do certain things

& pretends not to do certain things

there are ways in which literature is not clean

is not sterile

is not outside of itself

is not existing in a way that matters so fully

there are ways in which writers pretend to do certain things &

    also don't do these things

like

writing about the riot from the 25th story

flicking the lights of a hilton hotel room on & off

or writing about the riot from a youtube video

the audio cutting in & out

or writing about the riot from the livestream

the screen glitching out into pixels

or having band practice during the riot

the guitar turned way up

or doing something really annoying & conceptual during the riot

i should be careful b/c this is starting to sound like some macho manarchist

riot or die manifesto

but rly

i'm trying more to complain about how the riot gets more imaginative
attention than physical attention & how those people doing the
imagining but not the attending

get the most IRL attention

the most visibility

but that only about 20 people showed up to J's sentencing last
Thursday

while someone with 1,003 facebook friends wrote poetry or papers or
reviews

that probably more than the 20 people who showed to J's
sentencing last Thursday

will read

it's really coming back to this black panther vs BLA line of can we even
think of arts as a form of militancy—& i'm very much conflicted on
this too

like i want to & i do but also with the understanding that it's not enough
& really has to arrive out of a moment of upheaval or conflict or
feeling & can't actually be predictive

that's why the fighting phase

that's why i'm not sure i trust the fighting phase

maybe it made more sense then than it does now

I STARTED OUT THIS PIECE

I STARTED OUT

I STARTED OUT BY TRYING TO INHABIT FANON
I STARTED OUT BY
TRYING TO FIGURE SOMETHING OUT

it's easy to think the poet is the problem
but the poet is really just sad or maybe
even just nothing & the poet can't
burn down J's cell or the entire prison
or all the prisons & the poet can't even write
a fanonian poem because what would that actually look like?
the poet can show up sometimes or not
the poet can watch
the poet can write, or not
because what would the fanonian poem even be—
it wouldn't even be a poem or a phrase or a piece of art
in the middle of the street
it would just be fire itself

WOULDN'T FANONIAN FORM BE SUCH A GOOD ALBUM
        NAME

it has the same problem still tho
tapes to set yr tape player on fire
light it up, light it up

visual disruption really feels like it does something
or opens a possibility to inhabit public space

beyond the body
like a puppet or a performance or capitalism's coffin
it's nice to have a task sometimes
like carrying gauze or glitter
something outside of yourself that participates
beyond the body
part of the mess of holding each other
together & staying out there
even when it's scary or fucking cold

nobody had anything & then suddenly everyone had something a
memory a moment a body feeling an adrenalin crash a terror inside
them a string tangled around each of our fingers holding us a little
bit more together

WOULDN'T CRASH TERROR BE SUCH A GOOD ALBUM
NAME?

i thought i could write a poem of each fanonian poem phase
one for assimilation one for nostalgia one for the fighting phase
i thought about doing it in a gay way i mean assimilation is so obvious
but like being confused & bisexual
& 18 with kind of medium length frizzy hair & one cool denim blazer
& trying to be a slut but boys are actually such awful kissers
so it involved a lot of studying & a lot of drinking & a lot of fake crushes

WOULND'T FAKE CRUSH BE SUCH A GOOD ALBUM NAME

& then it shifted to nostalgia no more bad boy kissers & just one
bad boy who rode a sexy bike
i always think i liked the way he rode a bike more than i actually
    liked him
but he had a long term gf so we were really 'just friends'
there was the women's center & of course the problem of dating
another bisexual girl or maybe by this time we had all moved into queer
or maybe it doesn't actually matter because the girl was your
co editor & summer roommate & always invited the awful kissing boys
over to our room while i listened to a lot of tegan & sara & studied for
the MCAT & went on long runs around the reserve. outside it was
    summer.
inside it was a fucking mess. & there was order at the women's center
a framework of understanding feminism

WOULDN'T FRANTIC FEMINISM BE SUCH A GOOD ALBUM
    NAME

but this framework always felt so frantic & i was never fully a part of it
bc i hadn't started there i had started somewhere else & i never
fully landed there which back then was totally frustrating
but now makes a lot of sense being surrounded by people
who were fully embracing their bodies & i was still living outside of
    mine
it's so hard to feel attached to your body these days
there was something always so dogmatic & awful about the whole thing

WOULDN'T AWFUL DOGMA BE SUCH A GOOD ALBUM NAME

we were tangled up in this stretchy web
in one of those awful looking new safety playgrounds
& my friend asked me what i meant when i said i still get
misgendered

WOULDN'T NASTY NETWORKS BE SUCH A GOOD ALBUM
   NAME

i'm pretty sure someone called u sir today said my friend hanging upside
   down
& i said when i get gendered at all
we hung from the stretchy plasticky robes
& imagined all the ways we could possibly fall out
of this tangled web how ever & ever we tried
we'd get stuck on a rope & another rope & another rope
before making it out or under really,
the whole weight of the web hanging above yr chest
there was no way to plummet to the ground uninterrupted,
like most falls we take

WOULDN'T BI-NODAL LOSS BE SUCH A GOOD ALBUM NAME

unless we just pushed off backwards & let go
leaving the realm of the webmess of gender
& trying to expand outwards before

our bodies thump when meeting the shallow mulch

WOULDN'T REV ROT BE SUCH A GOOD ALBUM NAME

like all the sounds left over from stockpiling
dumpstered food in summer
scraping out bread from under
gross meat packs in a steaming dumpster
dumpstering in the winter is so much safer
but so much more miserable
we can share
we can support the strike
we can show up
we can show up against
we can show up for each other
attracted to some & repulsed
by so much else
maybe even everything else
it's fucking overwhelming

10 to 20 people gather every thursday night
in a dark warehouse to write letters to prisoners
each session we write birthday cards for those
who have birthdays in the upcoming month
prison mail is fucking slow.
we passed cards around & double checked
which prisons would allow colored pencil

scrawls through the walls
anyone can write a letter at anytime
but there is something very sweet &
very awkward about doing this together
we pass birthday cards around
making sure everyone signs them,
writes a little note
just a little note for a very, very tall wall
J got transferred this month
so we write him a card
a little note
just a little note for a very, very tall wall
after everyone's signed his card
we notice that someone wrote
'happy birthday' on his card
even though it's not his birthday
we scratch it out & seal the envelope
just a little crossed out note for a very, very tall wall

if only i can find some way to approach the fight then
black out / an imaginary fire
then stumble into the aftermath
still with the problem of invisibility
still in the gender webmess
still with a very, very tall wall between us
still dirty, of course
light it up, light it up

WE ARE LEFT IN THE AFTERMATH
MAYBE WE TALK, MAYBE WE DON'T
MAYBE WE FUCK, MAYBE WE DON'T
MAYBE NEXT TIME YOU'LL SHOW UP

it's so hard to feel attached to your body these days
it's so hard to feel attached to the idea of a body that may never exist
it's so hard to feel attached to the idea of a world that may never exist
no matter how court dates & letter writing nights & meetings & demos
we show up to
we show up
we can show up against
we can show up for each other

I STARTED OUT THIS PIECE
I STARTED OUT THIS PIECE
TRYING TO FIND A GOOD ALBUM NAME
TRYING TO FIND A PROGRESSION FROM
MELTING IN
CROSSING OUT TO FADING OUT TO RAGING OUT
OUTSIDE TO INSIDE
PHASE TO PHASE
DWELLING TO REMEMBERING TO FIGHT TO AFTERMATH

WE ARE LEFT IN THE AFTERMATH
MAYBE WE TALK, MAYBE WE DON'T
MAYBE WE FUCK, MAYBE WE DON'T
MAYBE NEXT TIME YOU'LL SHOW UP
OUTSIDE TO INSIDE
PHASE TO PHASE
DWELLING TO REMEMBERING TO FIGHT TO AFTERMATH

AN UNBECOMING

imagine the possibility of singularity unbecoming

imagine the possibility of unbecoming

It is imagined because

A nazi who shot a protester in seattle is let out of jail within a
couple days

It is imagined because

A bounty is placed on the head of the person who punched Richard
Spencer on J20

It is imagined because

The gay face of the alt right is coming to Berkeley next week

It is imagined because

Civil disobedience just got banned in 5 states

It is imagined because

A mosque got torched in seattle on MLK day

It is imagined because

They have the $ $ to take us all down

It is imagined because

A bulletproof vest costs 400-700$

It is imagined because

I try to read theory but just think of you fucking me with your
    entire hand

It is imagined because we have yet to

imagine the possibility of singularity unbecoming
imagine the possibility of unbecoming

It is imagined because we have yet to articulate a collective desire

I think about the limits of what I will & will not do in order to stop this

I think about the limits of what I will & will not do in order to stop this
I have the limits of/what my body is capable of/what my body can
withstand/how much trauma I can absorb

I think about the limits of what I will & will not do in order to stop this
I have the limits of my resources/my networks/my friends

I think about the limits of what I will & will not do in order to stop this
I don't want to think about the limits anymore but I feel as though they
are not thought of enough

I think about the limits of what I will & will not do in order to stop this
but I don't want to think about the limits because all of us together are
expansive

I think about the limits of what I will & will not do in order to stop this
while a friend texts me & says she saw my mugshot from 2012 while
reading about the J20 DC protests

I put a rush on my FBI file b/c I need to know where I stand in all of this

Just a whatever singularity / collective spectator violence / anti-narrative / A CLOSED WORLD / A SOCIAL SPACE / Language as a community made out of signs / A PURE WORLD OF SIGNS / THE STORAGE OF TORTURE / Dissemination as colonization of the mind / WHEN THE RITUAL WENT OVERBOARD / B/C THE PHOTOS FROM ABU GHRAIB GOT DELETED / B/C OUR RELATIONSHIPS TO EACH OTHER ARE DOCUMENTED / BE WARY OF THE FRINGE

In order to transcend national boundaries I think

In order to transcend the limits of a whatever singularity I think

I think about wanting to document everything & how I also want to
    delete everything
I think about wanting to free up space to document new things
I think about wanting to document new things & how I have to delete
digital relationships in order to do this

I scroll through correspondence from people I have fucked before I
    delete them
I scroll through correspondence from ex friends before I delete them
I scroll through correspondence from ex friends that I did performances
    with before I save the photos & delete the text
I scroll through correspondence from the dead & can't bring myself to
    delete them

I scroll through the names of who is showing at SFMOMA & think about
how the wrong people get deleted & how art institutions continue to
support murderers like Carl Andre & forget people
who were actually important like Ana Mendieta
I scroll through public family records I have tried to delete from my
memory but am now trying to uncover & once I have finished scrolling
I delete them in hopes it makes it harder for the FBI to find me

A nation built up like a secret everyone knows

A nation built up on a global web of lives

A nation built up like powerwashers that clean cum off the sidewalk

A nation built up against a simple villain

I am the villain.

But how dare u think me to be simple

THIS MYTH

IS HARD

ON

THE

BODY

/ / /

I WOULD ABANDON MYSELF FOR SWEAT
FOR THIS LOSS OF FEELING / UP AGAINST EVERYTHING / AS
A WHATEVER SINGULARITY

People work for the US military to get visas & then get denied entry
after 10 years of service

Thousands occupy airports

I want to go to sfo but stay up too late & sit in the sun instead

PPL ARE RIOTING AT SFO
PPL ARE RIOTING AT JFK
PPL WHO ARE CITIZENS GET SENT TO PLACES WHERE
THEY'VE NEVER BEEN

I WAKE UP EVERY MORNING SURROUNDED BY DEATH
I WAKE UP EVERY MORNING SURROUNDED BY SOLIDIFIED &
AGGRESSIVE RACISM
BASED ON TERROR
ON THE PLACES CAPITALISM HAS LEFT
UNTOUCHED FOR NOW
PLACES THE TENDRILS HAVEN'T WRAPPED THEMSELVES
AROUND YET
HAVEN'T EXTENDED CONTROL YET

NOW THEY EXERCISE POWER IN A NEW BUT ACTUALLY
AN OLD WAY

I NOW WAIT FOR MY RIBS TO STRETCH & WIDEN OUT SO I
CAN LAY DOWN FLAT

SO I CAN SLIP THROUGH THE BORDERS & BARRICADES &
WALLS & SCREENS

SO I CAN SLIP THROUGH THE TIGHTENING ENTANGLEMENTS

/ /

I WAIT FOR MY RIBS TO STRETCH & WIDEN OUT SO I CAN
LAY DOWN FLAT SO I CAN SLIP THROUGH THE BORDERS /
WALLS / TIGHTENING ENTANGLEMENTS / TV SCREENS
FLAT GLASS MEANT FOR CRASHING THROUGH
PANE AFTER PANE
THE KIND OF MOMENTUM THAT NOTHING
IN THE WORLD CAN STOP
I'LL RUN THROUGH ALL THE GLASS PANES ONE AFTER
ANOTHER AFTER ANOTHER
& I WILL BE BEAUTIFUL
I'LL GET CUTS & ENJOY EACH & EVERY ONE B/C MY POWER
WILL BE MARKED UPON MY SKIN FOREVER
I HOPE THAT OTHERS WILL NOTICE THESE MARKS & BE
REMINDED OF HOW
I HAVE ENDURED
HOW I WILL CONTINUE TO ENDURE
I KEEP RUNNING THROUGH THEM SHEET AFTER SHEET & MY
BOOTS BEGIN TO FRAY / THE SOLES SPLITTING FROM THE
CRUNCH OF SO MUCH GLASS BENEATH ME MY CLOTHES
BEGIN TO UNRAVEL
I LET THEM
I AM BECOMING UNBOUND
I AM UNRAVELLING
I AM UNBECOMING
I AM TRYING TO TRANSITION INTO A WORLD W/O SO MANY
SHEETS OF GLASS TO RUN THROUGH

BUT HONESTLY
I DON'T KNOW WHERE TO LOOK RIGHT NOW
I JUST SEE A TRAP / OF ENDLESS SHEETS OF GLASS
STRETCHED OUT
BEFORE ME

/ / / / /

A nation built up like a secret everyone knows

A nation built up on a global web of lives

A nation built up like powerwashers that clean cum off the sidewalk

A nation built up against a simple villain

I am the villain.

But how dare u think me to be simple

THIS MYTH

IS HARD

ON

THE

BODY

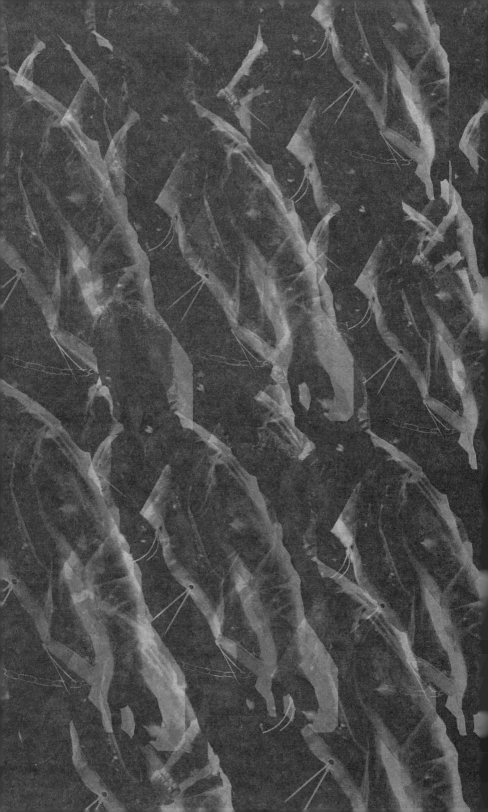

WHAT IS CLOSED/ WHAT IS CONTAINED

What does it mean to contain something like a piece of land/a country/a nation/a body like a pair of bodies/a pile of bodies/a set of words between two covers/a few fingers inside someone else's body/ inside someone else's mouth biting down hard/teeth marks across the knuckles/red indents you could throw on a scanner & still get a decent read/ decent image/decent pic/pic4pic/t4focusgroup/t4t/ t4fuckmeuntilimfinallyexhaustedenoughtofallasleep

What does it mean to contain an identity/to contain an I in one body/I think of my multiple selves/fixed against the wall/hooks around their necks holding them in place

All of my selves/contained in separate bodies/connected through the desiring machine/not through skin/all of these selves/contained in a room/where is the room/I see it floating in some dark abyss/hung in some static time vacuum or deep underground/blurred deep walled up with concrete/& then dirt & then a volcano so dark you think it will never end & just runs all the way through/it spans the whole earth

A BROKEN BOTTLE THAT WAS A LITTLE TOO HARD TO
SHATTER / A ROLLED CIGARETTE THAT BROKE OPEN IN MY
POCKET BEFORE I COULD SMOKE IT / AN EMPTY BOTTLE
THAT WAS EMPTY BEFORE I WAS DRUNK / A NOTEBOOK /
FULL BEFORE I GOT HONEST / AN EMPTY GAS TANK BEFORE
I ARRIVED / BEFORE I GOT FAR / A ROOM FULL OF PEOPLE
THAT EMPTIED BEFORE I WAS LOUD / A PROJECT THAT
FELL APART BEFORE I HAD A CHANCE TO HATE IT FIRST /
A SEASON THAT CHANGED BEFORE I HAD ACCUMULATED
ENOUGH RESOURCES TO GET OUT / EVERY FEW WEEKS A
LOVER / I KEPT GETTING SICK BUT COULDNT STOP KISSING
/ A NIGHT THAT WAS TOO LONG TO STAY UP FOR BUT
TOO SHORT TO SLEEP THROUGH / A DESIRE FOR ANOTHER
WAY OF LIVING UNRELIANT ON THE STATE / THAT COULD
NO LONGER EXIST TANGENTIALLY / EXISTING INSTEAD OF
/ ALONGSIDE A GROUP OF BEETLES THAT INVADED THEN
TOOK DOWN A GIANT POWERFUL TREE ONE TINY W/HOLE
AT A TIME / FINALLY COLLAPSE INTO EACH OTHER / CRACK
ANOTHER TREE FALLS IN THE FOREST & NO ONE GIVES A
FUCK B/C THEY'RE BUSY CARVING OUT THEIR OWN
W/HOLES THAT MIGHT COLLAPSE INTO EACH OTHER SOME
DAY TOO / I WONDER HOW LONG IT TOOK / THE COLLAPSE
/ I WONDER WHAT THEY WERE THINKING ABOUT THE
W/HOLE TIME / LIKE WERE THEY JUST HUNGRY OR TAKING
DOWN A SYMBOL OF POWER / THEY FELT NEEDED TO BE
TAKEN DOWN / like riding 911 trauma blasting sleigh bells / like
riding dirty on tour from tucson to oakland

ALL SEALED UP VERY TIGHT / THE SUTURED PULL ALMOST
TOO HARD / RISK SLICING THE VERY SKIN / IT'S SUPPOSED
TO HOLD TOGETHER / SMASHING THE SEPARATED EDGES
SHUT / SPLIT BY A VIOLENCE THAT HAS OCCURRED AGAINST
US / CONCENTRATED LIKE A LIGHTNING BOLT / DID YOU
KNOW THAT ONCE YOU GET STRUCK BY LIGHTNING ONCE
/ THE LIGHTNING IS EVEN MORE DRAWN TO YOU THAN
BEFORE / SOME LAW OF RANDOMNESS / AT PLAY

YOU'RE JUST A BODY WITH BROKEN SEAMS
TRYING TO HOLD TOGETHER UNTIL THE NEXT STRIKE

THE NEXT MOMENT OF CONCENTRATED VIOLENCE
AGAINST THE EDGES OF OUR INTERIORS
THE MOST NECESSARY EDGE WE HAVE
& OFTEN THE HARDEST TO HOLD
EVEN @ RESTING STATE
EVEN @ RESISTING STATE
RESTING STATE LIKE
WHAT ARE WE EVEN / WITHOUT OUR EDGES
OUR OUTLINES
A SOFT GREY PUDDLE OR TACKY CHILDREN'S CLAY
ROLLING UP INTO
A BALL / SMALLER & SMALLER

WHAT ARE WE EVEN / WITHOUT OUR EDGES / WITHOUT
OUR OUTLINES!

HOW DO WE MAINTAIN THEM AGAINST ALL POSSIBLE
VIOLENCES

HOW DO WE STAY W/HOLE

I THINK OF THE LITTLE CONNECTORS WITH TINY METAL
TEETH HOLDING MY OUTLINES TOGETHER

I THINK OF ALL THE STRETCHES & PULLS THAT CAUSE THE
TEETH TO BEND

I THINK OF EACH LITTLE METAL TOOTH BREAKING
AT DIFFERENT POINTS
DIFFERENT STRIKES OF ENERGY
WELLED UP AGAINST EACH CONNECTING TOOTH
& ITS CONNECTION

EACH CELL OF SUPREMACY RISING UP TO BLAST OUR TEETH
ALL OVER THE SIDEWALK
TOO SMALL TO GATHER BACK UP
I GATHER AS MANY AS I CAN / PLACE THEM
IN THE PALM OF MY HAND
I USE A TOOTHPICK WITH A TINY AMOUNT OF GLUE / I TRY
TO STICK THEM BACK ON / SOME OF THEM ARE BENT /
SOME OF THEM ARE CROOKED / SOME HAVE BEEN PUT BACK
IN THE WRONG PLACE
IT'S HARD TO KNOW / IF YOU DON'T PRESS ON EXACTLY ON

THAT PART / OF THE OUTLINE / WILL IT STAY TOGETHER /
OR SPREAD APART / ALL OVER AGAIN & THEN WHAT

EVERYTHING IS JUST TOO SMALL TO PUT BACK TOGETHER
JUST THE RIGHT WAY / SO WE BECOME THESE MUTANT
CYBORGS WITH SHORTS & SCARS & WELDED POINTS /
BUBBLED UP / RAISED CONNECTION POINTS THAT HEAL
LIKE TATTOOS DONE WITH A HAND TOO HEAVY
FOREVER RAISED FOREVER

A TEXTURE UNINTENDED ON THE SURFACE OF MY OUTLINE

WATCH IT BREAK
WATCH IT RISE
WATCH IT TRY TO HEAL
WATCH IT TEAR
WATCH IT BREAK AGAIN
WATCH ALL THE LITTLE METAL TEETH FALL OUT
RING AS THEY HIT THE SIDEWALK
& RING AS THEY HIT THE SIDEWALK

&
RING AS
THEY
HIT THE
SIDEWALK

IT WILL SOUND LIKE DORSEY PLAYING BACH ON
    STAND UP BASS
THAT SAD BUT FUCKED UP BEAUTIFUL KIND OF SOUND
WHERE IT RAINS & THE MAIN CHARACTER ON SCREEN IS
HELLA LONELY & PROBABLY JUST LOOKING TO LEAVE TOWN
UNLESS SOMEONE CAN CONVINCE THEM OTHERWISE

THE ACTUAL HOURS OF TENDONS STRETCHED AROUND
WRISTS HOLDING THEM DOWN THE CHAIR'S ARMS IN A WAY
THAT'S WET & SLOW & NASTY LIKE YOU COULD SLIP OUT
BUT YOU'RE NOT SURE THAT'S WHAT YOU WANT YOU KNOW
COMPLEX DESIRE
IN THE SLOW
HEAVY MOMENT

I GOT LOST/
I GOT DELETED

After *Covered in Time and History: The Films of Ana Mendieta*
2017 BAMPFA, Berkeley, CA

LIKE CARVE A W/HOLE INTO THE WALL

RUB AGAINST THE SURFACE

SPEAK MY NAME OUT

EVERY TIME YOU APPLY MORE INK TO YOUR PALM

I AM THE RED IN THE BUCKET

I AM IN THE RED ON YOUR PALM

I AM IN THE RED PASTED AGAINST THE WALL FACE

There

Is

A

Devil

Inside

ME

THERE IS A DEATH THAT HAUNTS THESE STREETS

WALK AWAY BEFORE IT'S TOO LATE

THERE IS A HAUNTING IN THE WAY

I RUB RED ON MY SKIN

THERE IS A HAUNTING IN THE WAY
I RUB RED ON THE INSIDE OF MY LEGS

THERE IS A HAUNTING ON THE INSIDE
I TRY TO EXTERIORIZE

THERE IS A THICKNESS IN THE RED
YOU CAN ONLY FEEL IF YOU TOUCH ME
RED ON SKIN

THERE IS BOTH A CALMNESS & AN URGENCY
IN THE WAY I WANT TO COVER MY ENTIRE SELF
IN THIS WAY I LEAVE THE GREEN SCREEN PARTS BLANK
LIKE
IF I BECOME UNCOVERED FROM THE RED
THE SPACE LEFT BLANK

WILL
BE
DELETED

I RUB MESSAGES INTO THE WALL
I RUB MESSAGES INTO THE WALL B/C I KNOW
SOMEDAY I WILL BE DELETED
I RUB MESSAGES INTO THE WALL

B/C I CAN FEEL HOW LOST I AM &
I WANT TO REMEMBER HOW I GOT HERE

SHE
GOT
LOST/LOVE

SHE GOT LOVE
SHE GOT LOST
SHE GOT DELETED

I RUB MESSAGES INTO THE WALL
IN HOPES I CAN BE FOUND AGAIN
I RUB MESSAGES INTO THE WALL
IN HOPES I WILL BE UNCOVERED
I RUB MESSAGES INTO THE WALL
THAT IS MY EXTERIORITY

/ / / / / / /

IF I STARE LONG ENOUGH I PRAY I WON'T SEE A FIGURE
TAKE THE SUBJECT OUT OF THE FRAME
WHAT'S LEFT THEN
AN EMPTY FRAME
OR A LOST SUBJECT
OR THE SMELL OF YOUR FRIEND'S SHINY BLACK HAIR
BURNING / TURNING INTO WISPS

MAYBE THIS IS NOT THE THING
BUT IT FEELS BETTER TO FEEL THAN TO NOT
SO TRAUMATIC RE-REMEMBERING
IS WHERE I'M HEADED WITH THIS

/ / / / / / /

THX ALIENATION / ANONYMITY FOR THE
PASSERSBY

THX CROOKED SIDEWALK SQUARES
FOR CONTAINMENT

DON'T STOP

YOU GOTTA GET 2 WORK

NOT NOTICING & NOT SEEING ARE
TWO DIFFERENT THINGS

/ / / / / /

FORCING ITSELF OUT LIKE A SPIRIT
I WAIT FOR AN EXIT
I WAIT FOR RELIEF
THAT FAILS TO ARRIVE
I WAIT FOR SOMEONE TO NOTICE
I WAIT TO BE STAINED BY EXPERIENCE
BUT NEVER TIRED
I WAIT FOR THIS SHOCK TO STOP
I WAIT TO FEEL SOMETHING NEW LIKE
EXPERIENCING SOMETHING FOR THE FIRST TIME
BUT I KNOW I CANNOT BE REREMEMBERED
I KNOW THE BODY CANNOT

FORGET TRAUMA
BUT I DON'T KNOW HOW TO ACCESS IT
I DON'T KNOW HOW TO GET BACK
THERE & I KNOW I AM AFRAID 2

/ / / / /

THE PARALLEL BETWEEN BODY AND EARTH

I DIG A W/HOLE TO FEEL ENCLOSURE

I DIG A W/HOLE TO MAKE A CONTAINER FOR THE PARTS OF

MYSELF DRIBBLING OUT OF THE BUILDING & ACROSS

    THE SIDEWALK

I DIG A W/HOLE TO FIND A DARKNESS

I CAN FALL ASLEEP WITHIN

I DIG A W/HOLE & THEN BLOW IT UP

SO THAT I MIGHT FIT ALL OF

MY PARTS INTO IT

EVEN THE STUFF DRIBBLING OUT ACROSS THE SIDEWALK

I NEED TO FIND

ALL OF MY PARTS

FIRST

BEFORE I KNOW IF I WILL FIT INTO IT

I DIG A W/HOLE IN THE SIDE OF A MOUNTAIN

BUT I CAN'T EVEN REACH IT

I DIG A W/HOLE IN THE GROUND IN THE SHAPE OF MYSELF

BUT I STILL CANNOT STUFF MYSELF INSIDE OF IT

I DIG A W/HOLE MAYBE BIG ENOUGH BUT WHEN I LEFT

TO GO LOOK FOR THE REST OF MY PARTS I COULD NOT

FIND MY WAY BACK TO IT

I FOUND THE TRAIL OF DIRT BACK TO THE W/HOLE

BUT I KEPT DROPPING MY PARTS ALONGSIDE IT

I SEE SMOKE & THINK I HAVE FOUND MY WAY BACK

BUT WHEN I STEP CLOSER I FIND MY OUTLINE HAS
    DISAPPEARED
& I AM LOSING MY PARTS FASTER & FASTER &
IT IS BECOMING HARDER & HARDER TO
REPLACE THEM
THE BROKEN PARTS OF MY OUTLINE SIT DOWN ON THE
DIRT HAPHAZARDLY & WAIT TO RECONNECT
I JUST HOPE THERE IS ENOUGH OF ME LEFT

/ / / / / /

oh you know, dig me out

so i might climb inside

so i can split apart my ribs

& lay down FLAT

what's beyond the screen/what's beyond the scene

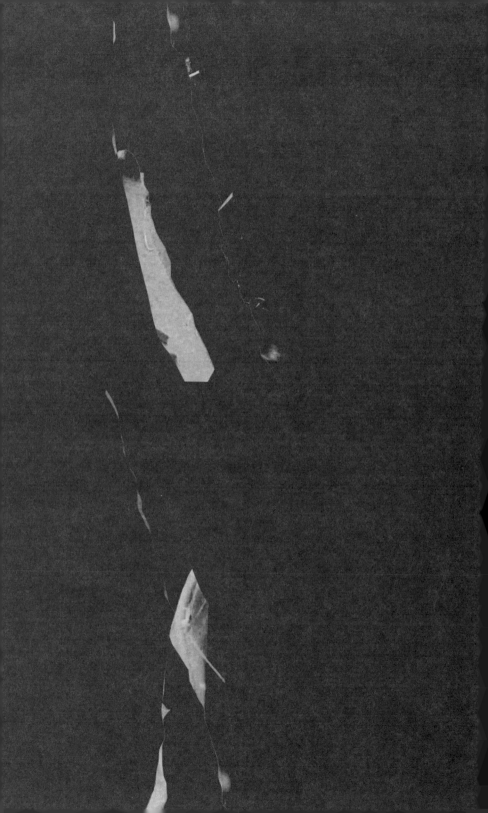

THE INTERRUPTION VS BLOCKADE

WHAT HAPPENS AFTER THE DISRUPTION?
BEYOND THE F L A S H P O I N T
WATER SNAKE
OIL SLICK
OIL SNAKE
WATER SLICK
SLICK SURFACE

CAN YOU EVEN STAND UP ANYMORE?

WHAT HAPPENED TO YOUR LEGS?

WHERE DID YOU LEAVE THEM?

IS IT TOO LATE?

WHAT DISFIGUREMENT IS THIS
WHAT DISFIGUREMENT IS LEFT
MY FACE IS TWISTED BEHIND ME
BUT I'M STILL NOT LOOKING BACK
I'M TRYING TO SEE
WHAT'S LEFT
OF MY BODY
I'M TRYING TO SEE

ALL THAT'S LEFT OF MY BODY
HAS IT ALL TURNED TO SAND ALREADY?

I LOOK BACK I TRY TO SEE WHAT'S
LEFT OF ME
I LOOK BACK I TRY TO SEE WHAT'S
L E F T
I LOOK BACK I TRY TO SEE
HOW I FORGOT
I LOOK BACK I TRY TO SEE
WHAT I LEFT OUT
I LOOK BACK I TRY TO SEE
WHAT I KNOW I'M NOT SUPPOSED TO KNOW

I LOOK UPON MY OWN DISFIGUREMENT
I LOOK UPON MY OWN DISFIGUREMENT
I LOOK UPON MY OWN DISFIGUREMENT
& HOPE OTHERS NOTICE IT TOO
I LOOK UPON MY OWN DISFIGUREMENT
& SUDDENLY REALIZE I AM BUILT OUT OF PARTS
I FOUND WHILE OUT DIGGING W/HOLES
THAT I WANTED TO FIT INTO
PARTS THAT I FOUND ON THE CITY SIDEWALK
TREES TOO BARE & DRY
SLUDGEY BEACH W/SOFT SAND
BUILDING WALL
FULL LENGTH MIRROR
TRAIN YARD
CRACK IN THE EARTH
RAINY MOUNTAINS
DESERT DUST

I

HOPE

OTHERS

WILL

NOTICE

MY

DISFIGUREMENT

TOO

I CRAWL INSIDE & PRAY I WON'T
FIND MY WAY OUT

I CRAWL INSIDE & COLLAPSE MY BONES
JUST SO I CAN FIT

I CRAWL INSIDE I DON'T EXPECT
TO FIND MY WAY OUT

I CRAWL INSIDE & EXPECT THE COOL OF THE CAVE TO FEEL
COLD AGAINST MY SKIN

I EXPECT TO FEEL A CONTRAST

INSTEAD OF COOL & SMOOTH IT'S WARM AND SCRATCHY
AGAINST MY STOMACH

I DIG MY FINGERS IN TO CLAW SOMETHING OUT
IN HOPES I'LL FIND A COOLNESS TO SINK INTO / BENEATH

I THROW MYSELF OUT OF THE CAVE & INTO THE WATER
BUT THE SURFACE IS HARD

I CURL UP ON THE SURFACE I HOPE I SINK & THAT EVERYONE
ELSE ON THE SURFACE CAN FEEL IT — THE WEIGHT OF ME
SINKING THROUGH — SLIPPING THROUGH THE SURFACE

BREAKING BARRIERS

SHAKING DOWN THE MAGNETISM B/W THINGS THAT ARE ALL
THE SAME STRUCTURE

//////

THE SMOKE RUNS DOWN MY OUTLINES
THE SMOKE RUNS DOWN MY OUTLINES
THE SMOKE RUNS DOWN MY OUTLINES
& BEGINS TO OVERTAKE ME

THE SMOKE RUNS DOWN MY OUTLINES

THE SMOKE LEAVES ME CHANGED

THE SMOKE RUNS DOWN MY OUTLINES
& THE RESIDUE OF THE TRANSFORMATION REMAINS CAKED
ALONG MY OUTLINES / THE SMOKE CONSUMED
EVERYTHING
I DIDN'T NEED ANYMORE

THE PART OF MY OUTLINE THAT WAS BARELY ATTACHED
    ANYWAY

THE SMOKE CAME THROUGH & OVERTOOK THEM, THE EXTRA

THE CHEMICAL PROCESS OF TRANSFORMATION HAS ITS
    EFFECTS

THE SMOKE RUNS DOWN MY OUTLINES & DISAPPEARS ME
UNTIL I AM DISFIGURED TEMPORARILY

THE SMOKE RUNS DOWN MY OUTLINES & DESTROYS ME

UNTIL I AM
DISFIGURED

THE SMOKE RUNS DOWN MY OUTLINES & DISFIGURES ME
UNTIL I AM TRANSFORMED

THE SMOKE RUNS DOWN MY OUTLINES & TRANSFORMS ME
UNTIL I BECOME A NEW SELF

THE SMOKE RUNS DOWN MY OUTLINES & TRANSFORMS ME
UNTIL I AM

WINGED

/ / / / /

I AM WINGED

I AM RED

I AM WINGED

I AM RED

I AM WINGED

I AM RED

I AM FLAT AMONGST THE OTHER RUINS

I AM FLAT B/C I AM

COVERED IN GREY ROCKS

I AM FLAT BUT I BREATHE ANYWAY

I BREATHE I AM CONTORTED I BREATHE I AM CONTORTED
I BREATHE I AM CONTROLLED I BREATHE I AM STILL

I AM RED

I AM WINGED

I AM RED

I AM WINGED

I BUBBLE UP IN THE SUN

I SINK INTO THE EARTH

MY DETAILS COME WITH ME

THEY ARE SHARP & THEY ARE SWEEPING

I STORE MY DETAILS IN THE EARTH

ALONG WITH THE REST OF MY OUTLINES

/ / / / /

I CAN HEAR THE PALM OF YR HAND DRAG ALONG THE WALL
RED INK GETTING TRAPPED BETWEEN YR FINGERS

I DRAG MY HANDS DOWN FROM ABOVE
MY HEAD / ALONGSIDE EACH OTHER / THEY DON'T
ALWAYS CATCH AT THE SAME PLACE / ALONG THE DRAG

BLOOD SIGN / BLOOD INSIDE / BLOOD OUTSIDE

DIG / DISFIGUREMENT / OUTLINES / CARVE / CRAVE

LEAVE BEHIND

DARK & DISFIGURED

CLIMB

INSIDE

A SCREEN IN THE GREEN
A GREEN SCREEN
HORROR MOVIE RED
PROJECTED INTO THE TREE TRUNK

THIS

SHOULD

NOT

BE

HARD

ON

YR

BODY

ABOVE & BELOW

INSIDE & OUTSIDE

CLIMBING IN

FALLING OUT

MY HEAD IS TWISTED BUT I'M STILL NOT LOOKING BACK
BUT IT'S STILL NOT TIME TO GO THROUGH I'M STILL

PARTWAY SUBMERGED

IN THE WRONG STILL

I'M STILL PARTWAY SUBMERGED

IN THE WRONG SET OF OUTLINES

I'M STILL

PARTWAY SUBMERGED IN THE WRONG WORLD
I LOOK UPON MY OWN DISFIGUREMENT &

SINK ALL THE WAY THROUGH

TEMPORARY /
AUTONOMOUS /
DESIRE

SMALL / MEDIUM / LUST

there's heavy & constant exhaustion
like widespread static
i lean in to the physical—
circadian shake & revolt
bruises dull & wide
thin pointed scratches
that grow loud with sweat
& a layer of uhaul dyke grime
buried deep in my knee scrapes + glitter + dirt + cum
dense under my nails
heavy & constant
when the cops kicked us out
we used their headlights
as a stage

there's something powerful about sinking into yesterday's wounds &
letting it all light up
my chest a fucking canvas
pay 2 stare up close & not through
any panes of glass
up close / & impersonal like
public sex is @ a distance
just bodies unforming
jaw tight

play

power

power

play

play party

(i almost missed my flight 2 go 2 that)

power situation / power switch)

cold-obsessive

all events are recorded

cold-obsessive

all options are recorded

cold-obsessive in which

bodies are mixed together against the purity of whiteness

sort it all out later

when the cops kicked us out

we used their headlights

as a stage

where the queers of color

whipped the white subs

/ / / / / / /

divisions & subdivisions & subspaces & low lit basements—that's where

we host meetings

2 avoid dangerous visibility—easy recognition—easy on the eye—
miss the blind spot—miss the heart spot / go back & apologize

b/w knowing & remembering where the cuts came from / where
      the structure
came from / where the walls came from / did you build them / did we
build them by accident / between ourselves / maybe i'm too hopeful &
people rly are that sinister

hacking & hacking until it doesn't track // glitter in the wind
the problem is
when u get arrested
with an X on yr id card
where do they put u?
actually
the problem is prisons
what if instead of collecting separate lonely individualities
we set them free 2 sink back into the collective

resist the present approach impurity
the exhaustion that happens through containment
what are the ins / what are the outs

send a drone to drop off a pair of boltcutters
i'll tie you up to the chain link fence after hours

dangerous mixtures—impurities rising

at once collided at once real & imaginary

all at once

what if we

just

all @ once

tore down the cages

1

2

3

SF PRIDE #1

after hours & hours of running up &
down SF hills
C said *This Is The Best View In The World*
this view
is the best in the world
driving back over the bay bridge on the lower level
that clip of skyline lit up brushing alongside us
feeling (dis)connected
nothing mattered / it all mattered
we saw each other / out there / a giant black & pink flagg
—ing hard up that hill on 18th w/ the tricycle sound system
we found a moment or many / daytime / fog adversant
the street wide & temporary / the lex boarded up & ripped open
for a second / u-locks rigid / how we all are in this moment
under daylight / the expansiveness
sad & temporary / climb this wall w/ me / it's tall but so are we /
stacked up against the wall / here we are / sad temporary

SF PRIDE #2: AFTER ORLANDO

i write QUEERS BASH BACK
on the garage floor in thick, hot pink chalk
it fades beneath everyone's heavy, jumping feet
before the end of our set
we were supposed to say something
i think i said something into the mic other than
the way u fucked me felt so good
something about demanding space
my mom calls, tells me not to go to
pride / that it's too dangerous / a terrorist
[white nationalist] might show up
i tell her i'm going to trans march & dyke march but
corporate pride sucks
this year—a lot more cops show up to pride even
dyke march & trans march
i'm drunk in the street
one of them pushes my friend
& my other friend flips him off
i wanna be drunk & not worry & just
cmon let us have this one afternoon where we feel
massive & that the city is ours & no longer tech hell
/ no one will ride electric skateboards & for just a few hours
we approach / a queerness in public

SF PRIDE #4

fucking courtney love on a dumpster

my fist
wrapped
in cum
& her
cum
dripping in to
the trash
beneath
was there
ever
a better
hybrid
her urging
while people
wait in line
for the club—
what do we
define
as public
—trash transfers
from private
to public

export

ubiquitous

problem

+ aesthetic

bliss

coming up

new &

inhale

dollskin

fucking further

into hollywood

fantasy

elbow deep

in Courtney

SF PRIDE #5

after dyke march
i went to the
hot   tub   orgy
a few days later
i got
evicted

HOLD MY HAND

in response to David Wojnarowicz @ the Whitney
(begun last day of the Whitney DW show 9/30/18, transcribed 11/11/18)

I

u made me want to get
fucked intensely & anonymously
hand slow, cock hard
    in bright, fall/en light
break thru the
gauzy exterior of
streetlamps @ the edge of
the water @ night
the kind that eclipses
depth perception making every
thing so much more immediate
amongst the lies the institution told me:
desxualizing intimacy
is a failure of visibility

II

the gradual interiority of

watching

someone flip pages & pages of

photos

of the one u/love

personal collapse/ slide in to icon

i wake early ready for

                        a fight

i wake early ready for

               a fuck

sometimes i think they're the same

gesture b/w us

the way the visual notebook

                  clicks

III

we sit

close but

& revel in this static of proximity

pressed up against DW's visual

mausoleum

people enter & exit

the grid—mid loop

we wait for the loop to repeat

anti linearity of water falling upwards

famous gays are only

pristine when they're

dead

IV

quick cut/off

V

we sit in between gallery walls
facing others
oriented transit parallel
recordings of DW sprawl out
along the tempered light
nonstop with the weight of
mortality / immateriality / hopeless rage
i want to grab yr hand
close the blanks between bodies
in present mourning of the decades
of queer bodies propelled toward death
by state sanctioned abandonment
air bears heavy
electric net of implication
in the next phase of queer hxtory
refuse the archive / demand the
                  immediacy
of extensions pressed sharp
we breathe the same heavy air
of rage pressed play
amps crackle with loss
loosened + looping

VI

coins cascade down on to

my face + brace for

impact keep eyes open

to see where the glisten lands they recoil

on my cheeks & my eyelids & my hollows—mirrored

each shadow holding a loss @ its corners

i let the elasticity of the screen stretch over me

taut & hope i can still breathe

i wield my queerness like a leather jacket

sexy & resilient

that fine, brutal line

b/w visibility & surveillance

but god yr spiked leather motorcycle heels

are turning me

on thru the window

of incomplete desire

these zippers make me wet

i bite my lower lip & make direct

eye contact with the cycles of production

until it grinds up against me

i reveal my hardness in the space left

between red suture drawing yr

lips together blood & cum form

rivulets down yr chin caught

by my tongue along carotid

i open up in heavy prep

to get fucked by late stage cap nonstop

for 8 hours feeling yr

hard cock @@@

then

frame—shift—click

VII

i love to watch the planes fly over NY

from my roof, light grids of

transit hanging low in the sky

cmon pick me up like u did

last night @ the leather bar

the shadows of anonymity

exceed identity politics

for a few hours

VIII

"xerox former self"

IX

quick cut 2

DADDY SANDMAN

& we all melted into hot water
like just before the boiling point
all hot water & skin & glasses of champagne
echoes of what we took from w/hole foods
@ the march so many times before
this is a different kind of march
we don't steal anything
just space on the street—temporarily—
that's not even ours to take really
we take it back from the city—temporarily—
overflow & widen
the vastness of us
uncontainable
by infrastructure or cops
we cascade through blocks & hills & 5 point intersections
heads thrown back in pleasure—temporarily—
@ the sight of our endlessness
wrapping up the foggy city
wide with desire
maybe it's candy or maraschino cherry
from the ground or a factory
trans*ported through the veins of global capitalism
to bob in each of our glasses filled w/
champagne we used to steal

when w/hole foods was still just a proud grocery store
before it became amazon's footsoldier
maybe it's candy or maraschino
stolen & carried through TSA
too much liquid (cum oozes from my filaments)
too many / / / (plastick surgery/overwritten anatomy)
still we made it to the party
knew where it was without
maps or cell service
drawn toward
chain to magnet
we know our ins are limited
daddy sandman
clicks through summer so steady

traces of pathways intersect
outer layers of collision
new circuits carved in skin
a freshly drawn geography
situationist sketch
thick scabs
more permanent than what
daddy sandman leaves us with
traces of desire's aftermath
sternal mold
a complete taxonomy of
each peak & every jagged edge

that adorn yr hands
all tearing at each other
we get a little closer
remove the millimeters of distance
skin affords
we exceed the limits
of daddy sandman's precise rhythms
forego sleep & eating
there's no time for maintenance
when it will all be over so soon
quick visit 2 our
fantasy harddrives
suspend certain n33ds
merge on 2 freeway
overdrive nerves sparking
network visible from within
bright links in the night

we exist @ the edges of this magnetism
for quite some time stretches out
occasional step toward temporary
network field abandoned building freeway
aneuryism where our fantasies are held
& finally
/rupture/
it manifests first as
a lot of texting & a lot of partying

a lot of incisions on the surface split it open
to the layer beneath
where our connections to each other
become more visible
turn on the blacklight
turn off the overhead

cables threaded underfoot
foot bones in feet adjusting to the
interruptions

turn off the scene light
turn on the stage lights

sharing is different than
what people take from you

sharing is different
than what the [_____]
takes from you

ligaments tighten
& calcify
against the brace of impact
& splinter
away from the concrete center

be
noise
clog
big daddy mainframe

be
noise
short out
the sandman
widen the clicks between
moments

skywriting that says
we want more than one weekend a year
where a mass shooting might occur

project on the side of the stadium:
the way you fuck is boring but you still don't get to watch

write in wet concrete
kick cops out of pride
or better yet
we make a world without them

draw in the sand on fire island
RIP Kevin Killian

spray paint
fucking everywhere
queer liberation means a world without prisons

dig into the surface of my sternum
hold my hand through the flash bangs
& i'll hold yrs thru the flogging
leather w/ metal studded edges
purple bruises
gridded nodes glow
in a mathematical array
of desire & resistance
i buckle my
bulletproof studded
vest
& melt in2
the mass

"POETRY AS FORCES"

AFTER CECILIA VICUÑA

*The "about to happen" / "poetry as forces"—when Cecilia Vicuña says that the
lies (the words, the language) of the Chilean dictatorship murdered & tortured
thousands of people I remember the power of the word & i remember the power of
poetry—"made of forces"—that holds something in the action of language—
material consequences can occur—not always—literal action is necessary but the
line between language & action no longer feels quite as precise as the street vs. the
aftermath—an emergence of literature—unrestrained*

i ask questions like

how to weaponize my own body

or what's left of it

how do we weaponize our selves

how to weaponize the poem words as weapons

give the poem teeth

overflow its vacancies

with sharpnesses

momentary, transitory

criminal aesthetics

an unpublished sketch

of affinities

explicit revenge fantasy

& pride orgy

accumulation becomes

a book

a constellation of bruises

a blockade

a dance party

on the freeway

alongside, from

within, erupting

out of

we sharpen

our teeth

& make attempts

glass breaking

disruption

simultaneous

ACKNOWLEDGEMENTS

I wrote the heart of *Villainy* in 2016 & 2017 during the most intense period of grief I've ever experienced: the wake of the 2016 Ghost Ship Fire in which 36 beloved community members were killed at a DIY show in Oakland, CA & the 2017 Muslim Ban that blocked refugee, foreign national, & immigrant entry into the US, particularly targeting majority Muslim nations. This book was an anchor & an outlet inside of a loss that I did not know a way through. Every day my thoughts are with those lost by & living with these violences.

I feel strongly that poetry can act as an accomplice to radical action & I am ever grateful to my friends, lovers, accomplices, collaborators, & enduring queer community in pursuit of survival and love through abolition: Andrea Marina, Adelaide Penelope, Angel Dominguez, alyn mare, Becca Teich, Binxxx Yglecias, Cecilia Vicuña, Davey Davis, Dawn Lundy Martin, Denise Benavides, Divya Victor, Dorsey Bass, Eli Dake, Ellis Martin, emji spero, Erika Hodges, Evan Raczynski, Hart House, Joel Gregory, Kamelya Omayma Youssef, Kay Gabriel, Lix Z, mai c. doan, Marwa Helal, NM Esc, Noah Ross, Rami Karim, Sahar Khraibani, Vanessa Butterworth & Zeyn Joukhadar.

Thanks to Juliana Spahr, Stephanie Young & Jasbir Puar for your friendship, mentorship & critical urging.

Thanks to Solmaz Sharif, Simone White & Eileen Myles for endorsing this work with your own words.

Special thanks to Simone White for selecting this assemblage for publication.

Deepest gratitude to Evan Kleekamp & Kim Calder for being the best editors I could ever hope for & to Evan for your brilliant design & vision.

Of course, special thanks to my mom, bo, & garcie.

Boundless thanks to the legendary Nightboat Books team: Stephen Motika, Lindsey Boldt, Caelan Nardone, Gia Gonzales, Lina Bergamini, Rissa Hochberger & Jaye Elijah. Thanks for being the best queer press for the freak poets to call home.

Many thanks to the publications where versions of this work originally appeared: *Baest*, *The Brooklyn Rail*, *The Capilano Review*, *Elderly*, *The Impossible Beast: Queer Erotic Poems*, *Mirage / Period(ical)*, & *Peach Mag*. Special thanks to *Commune Editions* for first publishing *THE AFTERMATH* in 2016 & making it freely available, as well as *nY* for the translation into Dutch for their issue on postrevolutionary moments.

Thanks, too, to the many stages that broke open for me to perform this work, particularly those that supported adaptations involving my body modification techniques of live skin-stapling, hand piercing & sewing: CounterPulse, El Rio, THE STUD, AAWW, Wendy's Subway,

Mizna, DRTY SMMR, YallaPunk, Publicly Complex, RAWI, (Be)longing Performer, Thinking Its Presence, Alley Cat Books, Codex Books, The Felt, & Center For Book Arts.

Special thanks to Juli Delgado & RADAR for the chance to tour for two weeks on the first ever all QTPOC lineup of Sister Spit in 2018.

Special thanks & expansive love to Lix Z for fiercely believing in my work & loving me amidst tragedy. Thanks for always collaborating & especially for taking the photo on which the cover is based. Thanks for pulling over at the Salton Sea so I could use the free McDonald's wifi in order to submit *Villainy* to the contest Simone White judged. Shout out to the red racecar during the aries season of that adventure.

In memory of everyone we lost to the Ghost Ship Fire. In memory of everyone we lost too soon by state sanctioned abandonment.

To Ara Jo, Nico Gogan, Kevin Killian, David Wojnarowicz & Ana Mendieta: I love you.

Author photo by Julius Schlosberg, 2020. Courtesy of the artist.

ANDREA ABI-KARAM is a trans, arab-american punk poet-performer cyborg. They are the author of *EXTRATRANSMISSION* (2019) a critique of the U.S. military's role in the War on Terror & with Kay Gabriel, they co-edited *We Want It All: An Anthology of Radical Trans Poetics* (2020). They are a leo obsessed with queer terror & convertibles. *Villainy* is their second book.

NIGHTBOAT BOOKS

Nightboat Books, a nonprofit organization, seeks to develop audiences for writers whose work resists convention and transcends boundaries. We publish books rich with poignancy, intelligence, and risk. Please visit nightboat.org to learn about our titles and how you can support our future publications.

The following individuals have supported the publication of this book. We thank them for their generosity and commitment to the mission of Nightboat Books:

Kazim Ali

Anonymous

Jean C. Ballantyne

Photios Giovanis

Amanda Greenberger

Elizabeth Motika

Benjamin Taylor

Peter Waldor

Jerrie Whitfield & Richard Motika

In addition, this book has been made possible, in part, by grants from the New York City Department of Cultural Affairs in partnership with the City Council and the New York State Council on the Arts Literature Program.